Snap

Templar Poetry

First Published 2010 by Templar Poetry
Templar Poetry is an imprint of Delamide & Bell

Fenelon House,
Kingsbridge Terrace
58 Dale Road, Matlock, Derbyshire
DE4 3NB

www.templarpoetry.co.uk

ISBN 978-1-906285944

Typeset by Pliny
Cover: lino cut by James Weir
Printed and bound in India

Foreword

The Templar Poetry Pamphlet & Collection Awards offers contemporary poets an opportunity to have their work published in pamphlet, anthology and collection form. Four excellent poets and pamphlets have emerged this year from the submissions, along with the work of over thirty poets published in the fifth anthology, *Snap*, a reflection of the excellent overall quality of work submitted.

Eight new Templar Poetry titles are launched at the 2010 Derwent Poetry Festival, four new pamphlets and the anthology alongside two collections and *Iota 88*. The latter is the fourth issue of Iota Poetry we have published since Templar assumed responsibility for bringing this superb international literary journal back to Derbyshire early in 2009, where it was founded over twenty years ago. The two collections are *The Beachcomber's Report*, a superb first collection from Paul Maddern, one of the winners of the 2009 Pamphlet Awards. The second collection is a new edition of Jane Weir's first collection, *The Way I Dressed During the Revolution*, shortlisted for the Glen Dimplex New Writers Award in 2006 and includes 'Poppies', which aroused a worldwide response following its publication in *The Guardian* in 2009.

Templar Poetry is committed to publishing excellent poetry, to widening the hearing and reading of poetry and to developing audiences for new poets and contemporary poetry. Further information about Templar Poetry and its work is posted on our website, where full details of our list can be viewed. Our poetry titles can be purchased online, free of postage worldwide, and are also available from good booksellers. If they are not in stock please ask your local bookseller to contact us directly if they would like to consider stocking our books or Audio Poetry productions.

www.templarpoetry.co.uk

Contents

Derek Adams

Lea Bridge Road E10, 1979

A posh gaff once, twenty foot back
from the main road to London,
on one side stands a tyre warehouse,
the other Stanwoods television showroom.
The brickwork is exhaust black.
A single tungsten bulb shines
above the front door, a sign,
in hand painted letters The Jailhouse.
Triumphs and B.S.A.s line
what used to be a front garden.
Inside peeling wallpaper half hidden
by faded gig posters for Freddie 'Fingers' Lee,
the Wild Angels and Chuck Berry.
Sweet smoke hangs like fog
above hair long and greasy
or short quiffed, flat topped rockabilly.
The jukebox belts out Bottle to the Baby.
In the corner on all fours,
Eddie does his imitation of a dog.

The windows rattle and shake
with the hawked up roar,
the squeal and brake of the Road Rat's hogs.
Shouting they burst through the door,
revealing sawn-offs and hatchets

from beneath black leather jackets.
A blast, the jukebox spews glass
and shattered platters across the floor.
An 'Old Lady' walks in, piled hair dyed black,
eyes blazing like a witch.
Mary Quant red lips narrow and tight
as the denim skirt that clings to her arse.
Earlier in the Royal Standard, a tattooed 'Jack'
she passed round a coin filled pint glass,
someone asked how much for a shag out the back.
She scopes faces, points, turns on high heels.
Walks out followed by the Rats
and Loco, poor son of a bitch,
dragged kicking and pleading into the night.

Threads

Not a believer, no,
but some sort of fascination
leads me along the fly blown road
to Preveli Monastery,
to stare into a glass case
in the cool of an icon lined chapel
at this silver crucifix
that is said to contain
a fragment of the true cross.

That same thing took me
to Glastonbury to look
at the Holy thorn, that grew
from the walking stick
Joseph of Arimathea
placed in the ground.

And that last week brought me
to Knossos, to stand
in the blistering heat
looking down
into a black doorway;
imagining Theseus
entering the labyrinth,
fingering a fine thread.

Yuko Minamikawa Adams

Apple

I have mated with dozens of men
but I couldn't conceive a baby.
On a summer night, in my garden,
I fell asleep.
When I woke up, I found my shirt
and trousers torn off.
My skin was spotless and
crows were pecking my toes.

Next morning, dusting a skirting board,
I felt a sharp pain in my stomach.
I writhed and lay down on the floor.
After a minute,
an apple came out of my vagina.
Should I eat it? I couldn't.
I decided to sell it in a market.
A mother may buy and eat it
and she would conceive my child.

Yuko Minamikawa Adams

Key

Whenever I make a friend,
I create a key.
I write their names in my address book
and set out to mould brass.

I met a new secretary at work.
I stole a glance at her and
watched how she typed a letter.
It stuck on my memory.

I went home and incubated her image.
I made a thin key, mimicking her fingers.
I also made it jagged
to reproduce clutter of her typing.
I put a ring on the key and
hung on a hook
like hanging fish in a cellar.
I ticked her name in the address book.

At night
I stepped toward her house.
I inserted the key into the hole
and turned it.

Flush

A Brighton postmark smirks from a stack
of mail in your hall. Cards in your ex's
winning hand are tacked to the wall.
I wait standing as you shut down swiftly,
shielding your screen from view. Lover,
I am not what you expected today.
You are a screw guarding my move.
Trapped in your sights, I fix my eyes
on the white open light from the street.
When I ask for the loo you go first
to check. Strewn at my feet, numbers
on cards inviting your call; a run of girls
in careless script, your underhand trick.
I can barely force myself to piss.

Ideation

And why not?
The balance sheet argues a certain case.

My lover mocks the way I file a book;
the order against chaos that I keep.

I send stroppy emails. Colleagues complain
I'm brusque, abrasive and don't consult.

A man I met looked me over with disdain
until I crawled out of the space I'd made.

I have run out of family. I may as well
be dead, my sister said.

Today I find a single argument against:
this silent son negates my worst intent

with unimagined trust. His need for me
dissolves contempt and self-disgust.

Rings

These hands held their disappointments,
made a fist of them - amber, emerald,
twister, rune - each chosen alone
on annual trips with you.
I was running out of fingers
waiting hopelessly.

I wore them all when I left you –
drove 500 miles to find myself
in a loop tape on the West of Ireland
plying the rings of Valentia and Kerry.
It was like rowing in a circle
of hills, the long shadows playing.

Eventually I pulled over, stopped
on the Ring of Skellig; I pointed the car
at a crashing sea, two sharp fingers
of rock rising from it eternally.
Next day I bought a Claddagh ring,
my hands quiet on the wheel.

Mara Bergman

In Search of the Nilgiritahr

They hovered on the brink of extinction
once the British discovered
how tame they were; how, with a pinch of salt
they could lure them and then
ignoring those gentle eyes,
aim and fire.

They hop
from stone to stone to outcropping,
soft brown, ever trusting.
There in the hedge is another, and another
with its nimble young.

An Indian couple stops us
not wanting a photo, but water
and it is my daughter who offers the bottle
and the man who holds it above his head,
looking up at a sky that couldn't be clearer.

Wild Boards at Periyar

The park gates close at dusk – at six – and by six
    all tourists must be tucked behind hotel doors.

It's later than that now – we've stayed too long
    at the Aranya Nivas, where the receptionists

loaned us their computer to email home.
    We look out the window and rush out the door

into the fine grey powdery night
    peppered with fallout, covered in dust, the stars

beginning to blink. A driver offers us a lift; *we'll be fine*,
    we say. Our hotel is just around the corner,

past the information booth shaped like a turtle.
    But the light is fading faster, beginning

to let us go. When we enter a wood, the trees fizz with calls,
    our walk is longer than we'd understood.

A group of wild boars skitters across the road, avoiding us,
    heading deeper into tiger country.

Search Party

on the banks of the Kafue,
somewhere to the north of Chingola –
a boat club of sorts where we laid on blankets
and laughed about it – being there –
Zambia of ants, hippos, crocs…

The brash glare of the sun
could run us cold at times, remember –
at the point of a gun, secret night thievings
or the day a crocodile stole a son.

He was gone – slipped under - boy hunter
who'd paddled, rod-fished knee-deep
on the slipway.

A river-mouldy rack of teeth
had taken hold - ruptured skin amid a splash
and black hole of missed breaths.

Such silence then.

Graham Burchell

Fishing Zambia's Wild West

Where did we fish? How far did we tow
beer, boat, food and tent? I cannot recall
a first glimpse of the river, or its name.
Did we ever learn it?

I don't remember pitching canvas,
only lumps under its floor at night.

My mind pictures the anonymous river
from the way it carried us,
not as it was seen from its banks, except,
when being the season of rain, a storm crept up,

forced us to an edge; one, where wetter than fish
we pulled ashore at a bare place under trees.

We joked about damp circumstance until
disbelief when K.C. danced for biting ants -
and the other man, what was his name –
with a bark in his laugh?

Graham Burchell

The rain rattled;
shoved fingers between the branches.
Ants in a great rain I could not conceive,
yet they found me too, so I knew the snips
of tiny pincers that helped themselves
to my calves and thighs.
                  There, memory clouds –
reopens on bright fish strung through gills
close to bewildered eyes – round, like currency
for the bribe at a road-block on our return.

The Patron Saint of Remaindered Books

She haunts the bargain bookshops,
calls them to her softly, hears the faint
flutterings among their leaves;
as stray cats would purr and rub
themselves against her shins;

she gathers them, abandoned children
in a shanty town, living on scraps,
fighting seagulls on the rubbish heap,
ekeing out echoes of their rave reviews,
envying the few, scornful of best-sellers;

she garners them – a harvest-home
where every one is dusted, shelved
in the eternal dewey decimal.

Peter Cash

Green Venice

an elegy for Paul Bellion and Lorraine Glasby who
vanished near Lauziers on 16th August 1986

Le Cafe du Plomb is deserted. Talk
in the straggling village, though,
is of an English couple. Last week,
they laughed under that parasol
eating moules and enjoying red wine;
they were cycling to St Malo.

The proprietor of the produce-stall
stacks his cabbages and stays quiet.
Like Monsieur Dufour, he's heard tell
that the people who pedalled under his eye
have never been seen again.
The priest says that he knows why it

is. Down the River Niortaise,
innocents can become easily lost:
its labyrinthine waterways,
its unsolved anagram of paths
that peter to mysterious ends ....
Down its over-grown canals ghost

other forms who rode to grief
in endless summer weather,

15

bewitched or worse in alder-leaf.
Don't look now: *sur une plate*,
an unkempt man re-loads his gun ….
Wild fowl, fleeing him together,

pan-pipe overhead. Meanwhile, in the maze,
it's likely that Paul and Lorraine
get off to picnic in a place
that blackberry briars over-hang;
relaxed, they listen to the dogs
and wait for Azaria Chamberlain.

Wool

In the museum, five mannequins dance, draped
in black outfits of knitted lace and patchwork-
felt hung in designer tatters over black leggings,
white plastic feet displayed in balletic poise.

Their hands, in mannequin dance mode, stretch
long fingers in an elegant ache. Swan white necks
emerge from collar and neckline, shoulders set,
heads turned to catch my passing glance.

Next door I join a group in old wool kirtles, circle
round them, a slow church parade, raise my eyes
to the level of their high *faldur* headdresses, doves
perched with trailing tails of white veiled lace.

The wool of Iceland works in the face of the wind.

Fish

A low cloud day and Hunaflói stretched out,
the harbour walls scissoring the grey silk.
Down on the quay not much sign of life till
I round the corrugated corner of Eagle Brand
and into the fish shed: I am stopped by the blocks
of colour and light, a living Hopper painting.

In the unlit background a grey metal wall;
lower foreground, a white crate with whiter ice
half-covers a black machine – the icemaker, perhaps.
Right centre, a man with blue gloves tips water out
of a yellow crate into its fainter wet-floored image.
Left of him, a man with his back to me bends over
a rectangle chain of whitish crates, fish black
and white just visible; he stands, black-booted
on the reflection of his orange over-trousers,
his left buttock painted white by the light
from the open door. That's in the frame but also -

the floor is blood and ice speckled, the piled ice
patterned by the fork-lift truck-tyre marks and in
the far crates black-lined catfish, spotted catfish
open-mouthed and disgruntled, the swollen pink
bellies of Arctic char, flat dab looking sorry.

Liz Cashdan

Now the story. "Here's a haddock for you,"
says one of the men. I take the plastic bag,
hold it well away from myself and walk it
back to our house. My friends will eat well.

Wound

I began with the spaghetti,
binding it round my fingers
to start a ball, like you'd spun it
on the prongs of your fork
before spearing the silence.

Then lettuce, spliced on
strip by limp strip. The cutlery
I wound on with pliers, rolled up
plates with the heat of my hands,
plaited them in with my watch

facing outwards as it met the ball,
stopped at 10.42. Then words,
yours and mine overlapping,
sticking as I pushed it
round the kitchen floor.

Followed by silence; skeins of it.
Then I leant back on the counter
and saw, the ball was too large
to roll out of the door.

Cover

I wear no perfume on days like this
just sandals and a dress that won't need taking off,
carry a bag into which afterwards I put
tissues, and the car park ticket
he peels from the dashboard and drops into my lap
when we get back in the car.

Leaving only bracken flattened,
which I tell myself could have been the deer
that roam, down wind and out of sight.
Only seen on warning signs,
silhouettes that flicker past
framed in red triangles.

A reminder of how they're apt
to make that one mistake,
step out, break cover, too late
to miss their stride-halting capsize
over bumper, bonnet and windscreen.

I sit more upright and nearer
the windscreen than I would choose,
but remember, (he reminds me as well,)
it would be best not to adjust the seat.

He drops me off but won't come in.
It's nearly time for him to be back
from where he hasn't been.

The Uluguru Two Horned Chameleon

waits
for David Attenborough to finish speaking
before demonstrating its
'incredible near 360 degree field of vision'
by swivelling each eye independently.
A stunt I have not yet perfected.

My mother rights the coffee table.
      My aunt sticks triangles of sandwiches back together.
            I lie cross eyed, shunned and winded. The cricket
                        appears
screen left.

This is the clip from the trailer.
We all wait
for David Attenborough to finish speaking,
   then the Uluguru two horned chameleon catapults its tongue
                one and a half times the length of
                  its body and reels the cricket

back into its mouth
               in   slow   motion.

John jokes the cricket should've seen that coming.
My aunt considers it unsuitable tea time viewing.

I am not in a position to argue.

My tongue lies pink and glistening
  over the occasional table and my aunt's crossed ankles
    falling short of the last egg and cress sandwich and my
          mother
     who has that look I last saw when I sat down
      cross legged on the floor in that skirt
       that doesn't reach my knees at the best of
          times
       opposite John
        when he was just her friend from
          work.

Her glare sends my tongue rolling
all the way back to me.

The Uluguru two horned chameleon waits.
David Attenborough has finished speaking.
Everyone is staring at the credits.

All of us including the cricket concentrate
on forgetting this ever happened.

The Not-Unlikely Prospect

with this frantic lovemaking
we'll burn up
or live forever.

I've learned a few things:
how to get the tyre
off a bike wheel
with kitchen forks,

how to help my
smile with dental
floss,

      how not
to take any notice
of barmaids with their hints
of what Eddie thinks might turn out
to be love or lust

for him.

as for us,
this *durable fyre*
continues.

praises be, I didn't have
to wait in this world
>   *'until conk shells*
>   *turned to silver bells'*
before finding
the One,

>   or stand there
until the codpieces
in Hearne's chippie
went swimming back
to the River Ouse.

Close Moon

The moon's too close this week, an old curse risen.
Everyone is restless in the house, wakes early.
She sees her likeness in my brain and sucks it,
Jams it hard against the inside of my skull
Like a party balloon squeezed on a rough ceiling.
She pulls at the bulbs under the turf,
Breaks their winter sleep with wet dreams of spring.

This time she will keep on coming until
Her pale frown fills all of my window.
Water loves her most and will leave us first,
The rivers levered upright out of their beds.
Then iron. All cars will crave her, crashing
Into skyscrapers in the crowded skies.
Ships will break their chains, sail across the land
To take off vertically from mountain tops.

Then stone. Wells and mines turn inside out,
Their deep shafts become towers in her praise.
Soon she will blot out the sun. In the darkness
We will hear moors and mountains break away
To join her, until the earth's stripped bare and white
While she is dressed in seas and continents.

James Dufficy

Château d'Yquem

Hardly any of her songs
Go over three minutes.
But her hair, her hair
Is like cascades of blazing silk.
Who cares if her fingers
Are calloused, Galouise-yellow,
And her English non-existent?

Most of her songs
Clock in well under three minutes
And are about the rain or birds
Or the end of summer.
But who cares when her lips, her lips
Are sweeter than the sweetest Château d'Yquem
And her English non-existent?

Tim and the Golden Jacket

I bought it in New York
Twenty-five years ago
And it was much too large.
But the sales job was just too good
And I produced my credit card.

Of course when I got off the plane
Into grey Heathrow
It was much too flash.
Something I would hardly wear in London
And never get away with in Banbury.

And here I am,
Fifty years old
With a gorgeous wife
And two children
Who aren't completely stupid.

Fifty years and I thought,
What the hell.
I'll wear what I want
And now with my big, beautiful chest,
It fits perfectly.

Selective Mutism

Language is very difficult to put into words.
                              - Voltaire

In the light before sunrise speech waits, a stray dog
concealed in a dark corner. Nobody knows
where it came from but everything is in place —
the hyoid bone is buried under the root of the tongue,
the throat's pathways have been converted
to a crossroads, no longer can we force food
almost larger than ourselves
down our throats without choking.

Numbers have been discovered. Shapes and patterns
have leapt out of the dazzle of stars as if
they were coloured; cycles of months, years,
precessions are predictable; angles and distances
can be measured; men see the far side of the world
as if they had X-ray eyes; the earth's turning
measures the passage of time. Words

are not part of the universe but inventions of man.
Nature prefers the foot-talk of elephants, the growls,
hissings, tail-lashings, smiles, raising of eyebrows,
even the neck-wrigglings of hammer-headed sharks
their rare cries as untranslatable as music. Words
may be one of man's many disasters.

Objects are named. Put together
they leap into speech, a frog unfolding the springs
of its feet, hopping away into concealment.
Mistrust and apprehension lean over them,
a sensed presence, ending for ever
the wordless wonder of a child.

And all will fall short of the brilliance of joy,
the howling of grief, the sob of an infant,
the riddle of love that is better unspoken,
fall short of the dancing of bees step by step: —
Food is here, make a right, fly on, look for blue —
for the good of the hive,
with no trace of a lie.

Corporate Memory

Your old Bechstein lies on the tip
keys cracked, glossy with rain
body rotting, replaced

with yet another harp
in the corner of the office
aching, I like to think, for its strings

to be caressed. The double-bass
before that, the lute, bassoon,
trombone... nothing

seems to satisfy their taste
or can erase the day by day
memory loss. Each instrument

is heaved away before
leaving a carpet mark let alone
a sound. The turn-around time is less

and less. They watch me. I've become
some sort of unpleasant reminder
of *The Orchestra*. When they ask

I say: *I am a music archaeologist*
but I'm not sure I believe it any more.
And it only makes them cross.

Yesterday the boss's young PA
the one with almost perfect pitch
whispered: *You must publish your*

Memoirs of a Pianist.
I shook my head. *It's too late now.*
Mostly I get the day done

proof the manuscripts
eat sandwiches at my desk.
I have a new thermos.

I must return your metronome.
There was something else
I meant to say.

Wendy Klein

A Boat People

Hardly a surprise that they took to the water, these river folk with
their floating markets, their floating villages. Hardly a surprise

that picking up the oars of ramshackle crafts could seem like a solution
when six year old children can row their younger siblings, standing up,

gliding forwards, the logic of it, compared to our Western clumsiness—
travelling with our backs turned towards where we are going.

Here in the Mekong, they row to the middle where the tour boats glide
                                                                    among
the water hyacinths. They wave tiny bananas like bright yellow fingers,

their fruit of unimaginable sweetness, point with pride to the family
                                                    pineapples stacked in the stern,
show us how they are the ripest and best.

Painted on the bows, the eyes of their boats are fixed on us as they
                                                                    approach--
eyes wide open, to show them where they are going.

Hardly a surprise that we either buy or turn away in embarrassment,
fumbling for our cameras as if a photograph could make a difference.

Port Selda

I'm not sure. Maybe Egypt, or
Greece. Not backward, just ethnic. I
remember waiting for a ferry,
men mending nets, picture-book sky.

An octopus pulled itself from
its bucket, plopped like a mop.
Then I saw her, her bare shoulders.
A boy beside me paused, looked up,

whispered *Meesta* as she stopped too,
her pose so sweet my mouth went dry.
On makeshift tables men shared food
ignoring her as she walked by.

And I'd forgotten my camera.
The boy raised his palm, asked *Meesta?*
She'd gone, and my ferry was late.
Or maybe it was India.

The subconscious today

Inaccessible maybe, but not mysterious -
theory's moved on. It's a mess though -
go up the rickety ladder to look for something
and you'll find something else instead -
half a roll of wallpaper, a gramophone,
some shoes. Lots of shoes. But where's the key
to that mouldy suitcase in the corner?

Next time take a torch. That's your consciousness.
Oh, and some plastic gloves.
One day you'll get some electricity up there,
knock through a dormer window, make a study.
Trouble is, any theory's only an extended metaphor
that's sure to run out of space in the end.
If only you had a cellar.

Gaps in the Sequence

First, get permission, no that's wrong
first have the thought, no
first create the mind
and train the sort of mind that has the thought
no first impregnate the chicken
or do you create the egg – from what?

In the beginning was the mind
and then the thought and then
the word, a sequence of six days:
chaos before order
dark before light
sea before land
fish before horses before carts
before dinners for dogs before
bags to let cats out of before
humans. And then, no work in a
garden with plenty of food before
the thought that they might eat
the one fruit that was banned.

First, get permission – no
first have the thought, no
first create the mind, the mind
that has the thought that says
why not, the words that bring
the whole thing crashing down.

Overwhelmingly Silver

I'm in some basement-dance-floor-dive again
its walls painted black, its peeling painted stars

as everyone takes their final partner, and
the mirror ball spins in slow motion.

I'm sitting on one of the broken stools on the edge
ready to sit out the predictable 'Lady in Red', when

a silvery haunting voice begins and I start spinning
drawn to the centre by a shimmering man –

his next-to-last choice for a one-last-chance
at the one-last-dance.

Teacher

Parking the aging Harley just outside the gate
he had already stopped the waitress, ordered
his cream tea, before he started to unlace
the embellished helmet, shake out a long grey beard
with grizzled shoulder curls.   So then he sat
at the adjacent table, smoothly slipped into
our conversation and soon switched its tack
to tell us how he once had been an artist
but relinquished that for science teaching
 - suiting what the system seemed to need.
Long 'out of the trenches' now, since reaching
his retirement, what he pursued today
was psychotherapy, also employing
minerals and crystals.   When probed politely
he offered a bland explanation, alloying
standard unspecific affirmations -
'more things in heaven and earth' - with cautionary
qualifiers, then encouraged you
to sense vibrations he was sure would carry
through your forehead from a diamond held
two inches off: with no success.   He fell
back on a garbled version of a programme
we had also watched, but had to tell
him we had understood quite differently.
Digressing then on energies that flow

from forefinger to thumb, he posed 'an ancient
Buddhist gesture' - so he told us - though
to me looked more the over-scrupulous celebrant
at Mass.   Perhaps beginning to run short
of subjects which allowed him to sound quietly
oracular, he told us how he thought
it was impossible to live in London -
a premise that was based upon three years
at Surbiton.   It would be a waste of time
to argue, given the difference in our spheres,
and so we just assured him of the pleasures
of the Elephant and Castle. A phone
was ringing in his bag. We quickly said
goodbye and left him to his second scone.

1962

My mother, forever Jackie Kennedy,
flicking her eyeliner with an expert hand,
dusting just the right amount of rouge.
Sitting in front of that curtained kidney
dressing table, in her satin Maidenform bra
and matching pale pink cami knickers.
I am two, helping her fasten her suspenders
onto her stockings, my fingers stumbling
on the rubber dimple which must somehow slide
 the American Tan nylon into its metal harbour.
I am bathed and ready for bed in my barred cot
and she is a bird of paradise with the aviary door
open before her.

Her lovers

Before we take this further,
there are three things you should know.

First: at your left shoulder
are my five lovers.

Dave is slapping his palm
with a baseball bat.

Günter has the eyes
of my younger daughter.

Blond Benedict
cannot speak above a whisper.

There is poor Nicholas:
sad how thin he got.

And lastly Roberto,
tugging at his shroud.

Second: my mother has webbed toes
and a single figure handicap.

Third: well, we already know
about all that.

I am innocent in law.
Come. Kiss me, darling.

I wonder what the Japanese
for *Top Withens* sounds like

Today a 67-year-old woman
from Nagasaki wept

on my shoulder, sobbing out to me
her longing to stand here since,

age 13, she had devoured
Wuthering Heights, hearing

the moor wind, and Cathy's longing,
in the sound of Shinto temple bells

and the parping traffic
on the Shianbashi road.

We stand today, my arm around
her tiny waist, as she dabs her eyes

and smiles and smiles
and we listen, together,

to the bubbling trills of curlew above
and the heavy breath below of

The Keighley and Worth Valley steam train
and to Kate Bush warbling from the Bronte Balti House.

I pull my blissed-out companion
onto the narrow gritstone pavement

as gaudy mountain bikers judder
down the cobbles where cholera flowed

in Branwell's day, and the apothecary
didn't sell retro pinnies,

but raw opium to ignite his dreams
of knocking his sisters' talents

into an early grave.

Another box of nipples arrived today

The hospital computer's gone mad
– that's the third box this week.
You stick them on the fridge door,
the phone, the handle of the kettle.
And we laugh. Then you are sick again.

This evening you sit in your usual chair
in the bloat of chemo, your breath really
bothering you. And me, if truth be told.
You are darning pullovers neither of us
ever wear – and even Oxfam won't take.

What if I could give you a new pair?
That will always pass the pencil test, even
at 90; with winking dark aureoles
and pert tips that tilt cheekily, but
don't show through your tennis dress.

You are muttering about camels
and licking the thread for the nth time;
specs half-way down – in your usual chair.
I don't see hacked-at womanhood,
that you've sobbed salt-herring barrels for.

I see you. Darning your way to normality.

From the Rev. Patrick Dineen's
Irish-English Dictionary of 1927

A damp green stretch of ground, as over running water
A little corner or patch of land
The colour of the bog
The seven concerns of the mountain
A little hollow; honeycomb found therein

Anything hollow like a cow's horn
A name for a cow with small horns bent inwards
It looked well for the cow
A unit of monetary value equal to three milch cows, especially
                                             in estimating fines
The sturdy calf that used utterly ruin the harvest
I slaughter cattle clumsily
Handling or managing horses
She is not a one-year old but a two-year old ewe
A she-goat in her third year
Having short ears
Call to frighten away a cat
May you not have the memory of the deer

The reaping-hook is now gone out of use
A heap of potatoes
A potato-cake; a frost-bitten potato; a stubborn horse
The heart of cabbage

Poor though worthy; pitiful
The instruments they used in torturing souls
Hemmed in between the enemy and the sea
Hanging today, trial tomorrow
The wheezing of death is in his throat

Companionship
Drifting, enjoying life
(Spent) on drink
Woe betide this poteen
Was it not great inventiveness on his part to make up such a tale?
He devised strange surnames for them
His eloquence outweighs his learning
In literary questions
The literal as opposed to the figurative meaning
State of being well-educated; propriety of manners; conceit,
foppishness
Poetical inspiration; the act of dreaming, seeing visions

A red-haired woman having a shade of red in her complexion and
exhibiting the marks of smallpox
The cynosure or model of all Irishwomen
A maid with beautiful hair
An invitation to kiss
She has completely withered my heart

Catherine McLoughlin

I did not deserve such ill-treatment at your hands
I suffer something without knowing the reason why
Sorrow, melancholy, loneliness, lamentation, grief, regret
(something lost, gone or absent), homesickness, pining, desire,
                                                    sensual desire

God is your debtor
Our championing priest
I turn Protestant
I am fairly well

Land of the Free

My father resisted family pressure
to choose the land of the free,
crossing instead to the coloniser,
but not expecting English children.
Hearing us speak, he looked
as if there had been some mistake.

Cramped in Mancunian suburbs,
we found American cousins exciting,
but wondered what they were saying.
We did better with song lyrics:
when they defeated us
visiting uncles could translate.
Reserved children, we rehearsed our questions,
urged one another into the room.
What was a Chevy? What was a levee?

I had remembered those questions
but not the answers,
until some underfunded levees
were fought down by the hurricane,
leaving American cousins as free
to go anywhere as the homeless are.

Catherine McLoughlin

Imperfection

By the Ligurian water,
a woman held out to me, standing alone,
a pink-white peach.
It was, I saw, bruised, diseased,
but only in parts, which I pulled away
to bite into the fragrant, juice-soaked creaminess,
rediscovering peaches, even fruit.

Which made me think of you, as things do,
whom I couldn't pull deftly to my pleasing.
Indeed, I failed to see, hurrying in Notting Hill,
gift or blemish, but swallowed whole.
This made me rather ill;
but bland, faultless peaches
now dissatisfy me too

In Absentia

He arrives suddenly in my dreams to hold me,
and is closer and gentler than he was
or wanted, when we were bodily there, to be

(in fact it was mainly a sighing acceptance
which his eventual departure aroused
rather than any long and raw incoherence -

perhaps the reason for these visits fathoms down,
this calm and regular reappearance).
Each dream ends, though, with a fast haul out

to the dull air, which, with unrelenting presence,
through waking hours and lighter sleep, hurts emptily,
has me paralysed, nauseous, cramped with numb pains.

Killarney Fern

It was winter when we looked for a garden,
wanting the scent of rained-on ground. Empty beds
were staked with labelled stubs, snowdrops
clumped beneath a statue blooming algae.
One grapefruit still hung on a tree.

I drew you into the greenhouse
where a jade vine dripped, unscrolling
from the sloping roof. The weak sun passed
through clouded glass, seeped into a gulley
shawled with moss - and there we found it:

frothing in a damp corner, shade-loving,
a fern as delicate as curling parsley.
It freshened our fingertips with a cool leaf-breath,
all the rare pure green that comes
when something living feels a shift of light.

Isabella Mead

Txt Msg

The embankment cradles the spindle of the track
as the letters flick up one by one on the screen.
Head against the window, I pare down my love for you,
calculating characters and consonants.
The commuter opposite jabs at his laptop in time to emphatic
ticks of his watch. And the kid next to him
teases a tabby-cat hunched up in a carry-cage.
Crammed in two seats, three women talk
in exclamation marks: pinpoints
through the drones of iPods and overhead wires.
Beyond the window, lights of towns scatter
and hills blur into distances
where the wind mouths out vowels

Isabella Mead

Peruzzi's Room of Perspectives,
Villa Farnesina, Rome

The room is empty. On the east side,
there is an open balcony. The other three walls
are painted as its exact reflection.
A colonnade stretches around

all four sweeping sides of the room,
supports a vast blue ceiling of sky,
the pillars so rounded that their sides
are calling out to be traced by the hand.

Lambent light radiates from all four walls
while the sun fidgets with movement to the east.
You could move easily between the columns
and flow out to the balconies, stare beyond

at the same blue sky, the sluggish sun
arresting in gold a configuration
of tiny crowded rooftops, laundry,
glazed rivers and valleys; you could imagine

the calm monotone of Mass, or a late greeting
echoing out across heated flagstones.
Yes, you have the choice of all four directions -
and, as you step forwards, is this tangible:

the deep toll of a bell, the rush of pollen,
the murmur of pigeons and placid water,
the surge of oxygen? Test each one.
There are three out of four chances of heaven.

Pat Murgatroyd

Scaredy-Cat Traveller

You come across yourself in the most unexpected places;
Montserrat for instance when you are searching for something
in the briefcase that you didn't have time to clear
before you came. You threw in your lap-top, some papers,
trusting you would have the skills to pull off the project.
You didn't really want to do it.

Pull out the laptop, spare discs, memory stick, then,
lodged in the front pocket of the case a two-year-old ferry
ticket,
timetable for a journey you never took, receipt for a taxi ride,
Falcon Cars Portsmouth, but you can't remember where to.
You are here now, anyway.

There's copy of a conference paper you were proud of,
the company badge you are obliged to wear, the baggage label
warning that gates close 30 minutes before departure.
In career terms this is the equivalent of closing gates.
You chose to be here.

From a well-known bookshop, a red star collectors card
- the lack of apostrophe makes you wince - is exactly
what you need for the opening address in the morning.
Top Tips for Reading to Children it says on the back.

Pat Murgatroyd

Mosquitoes are biting, volcanic ash is gritting every surface,
roughing up your tonsils, but you came to help.
You are glad you're here, aren't you?

Glamour Who's Who

What is it like to be you? he wanted to ask.
Under what name do you go?
What do you do? as they say.

There was a note of swagger in his entrance,
a touch of swag in his gear, jacketed,
jeaned, bright scarfed, ready fruit on stark display.

I watched eyes in the crowded room sharpen.
Here was a cartoon before me, with a
dash of Hogarth to smash at civility.

He chewed meditative gum, eyes down, sealed up.
A hint of brute scowl disfigured his mouth.
This was one from out of doors, wild, farouche.

More questions buoyed up the expectant air.
Where do you live? What fills your mind?
What is solely you in this solitary world?

'How are you?' acquired a new meaning.
'I would like to know you' caught an old one.
What vastness to be privy to his pleasure.

Pick-ups

Bringing a stranger home
is an old dream. Tease, lure, pluck her,
or him, choice from the street. The dream
persists, despite the years,

despite the failures. I have seen the faces:
such suddenness at my unfamiliar door:
it is like walking the plank, or some of it,
thrilling.

So, before I leave the house, I check its credentials.
No scary objects, no shameful smells,
no stray poems or incriminating diary,
no final demands or an unmade bed.

And then it›s the long self-motivated streets,
as public as law-courts, swirling like a fairground.
I judge them fast, the candidates, inside the flicker
of their passing, the quiver of my need.

It is owed a surprise visit, the bare and patient house.
There was a Dutch boy disguised as a tourist;
there was a skinny girl in stark white
with nothing to say. But they stayed a while.

Otherwise, over the years it›s been a disappointment
for the house. Big blank voids
punctured like a forbidden tattoo on the air
unstirred by movement other than mine.

Angry

He did not show this by the way he inserted
the knife into the hot apple and split

it on the flat wood with a bang; the way he
pushed the iron pole they used to stoke the fire

deep inside the spitting twigs, the twisted news
print, timber beams, white dust. Instead,

he withdrew from her before the height
of it and he lifted a finger to the window,

to the inclement glove about their house,
flapping to come in. He peeled the duvet away

slowly, drawing heat from the flesh
just as you'd freeze-dry meat or fresh fruit.

Time

Against a stethoscope,
even the hum of a rodent's heart
can be divided into its constituent beats
and the gaps between.

Considering this,
we bought a camera, set it on a timer
shot our life for sixteen seconds, printed
ten thousand frames

on photo paper,
pasted them to the bedroom wall.
We put the camera on the fridge to cool, split a Cobra
into two stemmed glasses

and searched
so near to the wall we could taste
the air clinging to it, feel our breath condense,
in each shot

my wrists
locked behind your neck, the same bottle
of sambuca on the coffee table,
the door slightly ajar –

each frame
identical to the last, as one heartbeat,
displaced inaudibly,
by the next.

The Buffer Girls

Jane is making *Angel Delight* in the kitchen. Say hello Jane.
It is as pink as her cheeks in concentration. Though this wavers.
Her lips pushed in a moue for *Moulinex*. Those blades like karate.
She watches, out the window, a bird flying up. Her hair cascades.
It binds tight and brown on pink blancmange. The whip is instant.
She has a bald spot the size of a thumbprint. Just like Mam.

Mam took imperfections from steel cutlery. Sheffield's stainless.
The dents were pressed against a grinding wheel. Knives with shine.
She had brown paper clothing, a handful of oiled sand. Sheer grit.
She protected her thumbs with knuckle rags. Once clipped one.
It took her hitching finger clean off. Nowhere to go then.
These days, the stub is grown smooth. Like the youngsters.

Now her granddaughter cleans spoons in the kitchen. Twice as fat.
Her limber fingers, fit on mobiles, stroke a number. It's ringing.
She books an appointment, Friday next. Manicure, facial, wax.
They'll perfume too, for a special weekend. Some muffled laughter.
She wants hers the shape of a love heart. The colour of Union Jack.
Under city lights, she'll be plucked and buffed. Say hello again.

Sarah Roby

Girl in a Lay-by

And so another pulls over at the elbow in the road
where he is drawn by the girl with no fingers but a fist
and a thumb like a slim, white candle which has no tip
but tapers off into the night as he winds his window open
and asks *where to* and she answers with a square
of torn rough cardboard held at the end of wrists
so thin they have grown down to keep them warm
but the sign is blank so he says *jump in* and she says
no with a one-two shake of her head and he pulls away
bemused but not the first as there have been do-gooders,
jokers and conquerors before him promising to take her
to somewhere well-meaning, to nowhere fast or who
swear undying one-night stands if she'll just get in
but now a man is cycling towards her who can offer
no lift and who wobbles on hills but never falls off
and who takes out a red fountain pen and writes
on her empty sign and she smiles halving her face
with a new horizon as she reads *you are here.*

Ritual II

Secular living still needs ritual
and so we make our own from white paper,
a square, exact, smoothed in a valley fold,
scored with a deep crevice down the centre.
Two corners then drawn in one arrow head,
arched back and flat and blunted into half
until, over a mountain fold, wings spread
in a vapourless trail, sure as a dart.

Although, we do not always make a plane,
some days the regular bend, tuck and crease
give us a boat, fish, a Japanese crane,
unable to lift from the room with ease.
One time, we folded ourselves a windmill,
tall and waving, even when the breeze stilled.

Descent into Faro

'I like to walk the beaches,'
he confided as we started our descent into Faro,
his words weightless, the first he'd spoken
in almost three hours -
groomed, fragrant as Pears' soap,
napkin folded small as
a picnic sandwich.
When he leaned across, the airbrakes kicked,
the undercarriage locked.
New to Portuguese, perhaps he didn't hear,
or chose to let me think he didn't understand.
'Praias,' I said, pliantly, as we hit land,
'da Rocha, the dunes at Lagos, da Luz.'
He had teddy-bear eyes
and rustled like sweet papers when he moved.

Naming Apart

After she left him, her poems began,
missives addressed to
Old Lugworm,
Stinkhorn of the Woods, Chicken Skin,
in which she took her pseudonyms:
Betony, Germander,
Lily of the Valley,
Red Riding Hood –
mail-shot sonnets of woundings,
symmetries of leaves,
the night she found
an ear-ring stud of antique pearl,
the downy taste of apricot,
the sway of a dark boat.

After she left him, his letters began,
a verse invariably attached,
addressed to
Old Lop Side,
Motherwort, Henbit, Split Fig.
He called himself
Monkshood, Foxglove,
The Cowled Ferryman,
Tom Thumb,
praised the object of her disaffection,

told how love was airbrushed to the last follicle,
and why, in spite of the language of flowers,
the wisdom of forests
and the conclusions of fairytales,
they were better apart.

The Limit of Perpetual Snow

Nisbet's Plantation, Nevis, WI

Morning comes on with three or four boys in the kitchen.
They've been here a while, talking high, gentle, throwing
thin soursop slices one to the other, their sweet hands
stretched out, laughing as the yellow fruit slips and drops
to the grey teak floor. The cook barks and his eyes roll.
"Pull them shutters. Is the syrup on the tables? Juice, boy?"

"Too early for the butter, Clovis, do you see the sun, boy?"
This is the best time; the smells and sounds of the kitchen.
Coconut trees creak and fan out from the night, hot rolls
rest while the shift girls gather toast cuts in baskets, throw
gold crusts to Bananaquits. They love the sugar, never drop
one piece when they fly up like blue and yellow hands.

Cook wipes his face with the back and front of his hands.
One foot on a green corn can, he smiles in the shade as a boy
comes out of the cool room, carries thick white bowls of drop
scones and dishes of cut fruit. The girls reach into the kitchen,
hold doors for each other with one foot, white cloths thrown
over their shoulders. Violet lays out rows of sweet Danish rolls

and together we take in the ocean, take in the impossible rolls
of white horses on blue, the slowness of beach weed, my hand
as I lean from the pontoon to gather smooth stones and throw

one then another. Violet smiles, heads for the heat, the boys,
their games, the girls, their laughter, the cook and the kitchen.
She knows I'll stay here, skim stones in the sun. One, drop.

One, two, three, drop. Inside the reef, a pale blue boat drops
anchor, the crew spreads out, reels in sails. A girl swims, rolls
with the keel, then hangs on the ropes and calls to the kitchen.
One by one the boys come out, holding juice jugs in one hand,
they crinkle their eyes and laugh in the wind. The young boys
who came here from Spain? They loved the way the clouds threw

white on the mountain, like snow. They tried to climb up, throw
perpetual snow into the heat of the island, where the red drops
of Flamboyant cover crumbling walls of old plantations. The boys
gathered bunches of blossoms, wrapped with hibiscus and rolls
of palm leaf. These small flower parcels became gifts, handed
to friends like chicken with beans and rice from the kitchen.

I loved the sounds of the kitchen, the throwaway chatter, the boys
and their games; loved the girls and the smell of sweet raisin rolls,
dropped into baskets; I loved the taste of the sea as it dries on my
hand.

Night fishing

I have a friend who cries at night,
    says all kinds of things,
        like the next time her husband goes night fishing
            she'll lock him out.
    I want to tell her that she will be shut in,
            only her face gets sort of shut up too,
                jammed and so far past crying
            like the door to the beach house that swelled up that winter.

You remember, don't you?
    How we couldn't get it open till we eased out the hinges,
        how rusted they were,
gummed up with crystals of salt and flaked steel.

One of the bolts had shorn right off but for the life of me,
        I couldn't see where it had fallen.
Perhaps, and I want to think this, it rolled away
    through the threads of your mother's rag rug,
        slipped down through the maple boards
            among hot water pipes,
                a tangle of line, a salmon fly
                    hooked round a sand dollar,
            the skeleton of a sea-horse.

The jumping-off place

Sam's in the Quiet Room, struggling
    with simultaneous equations.
        Two doors
            sigh, swing open, bump closed.

Whispers that are not whispers filter from somewhere.
    "How's she doing in there?"
        "I'll check Mr Rosen's feet."
            "The grand-daughter called. She'll be in at four."

Mrs Clifford is in the Day Room.
    Her hair is browner than anything brown, only
        when she bends down, the light moves through
            individual hairs, to her skin.

It's a giveaway.
    She holds a copy of *Hello* magazine.
        Someone has torn off Catherine Zeta Jones' wedding dress.
            She lifts the picture close to her face, moves her lips,
                smiles at something.

Small oval baskets hold paper squares of tea.
    Organic Cinnamon & Crab-Apple,
        Country Cow Parsley & Rose-Hip.
            An urn bubbles up the corridor.

I follow it and the staccato business of the auxiliaries.
They squeak about in white crocs and short-sleeved overalls.
I don't want their attention,
but anyway.

"You want some tea? Sure, help yourself. The blue fridge.
The blue one. The fridge next to the green sign.
Hey, don't chuck the carton.
We tick-off the sell-by dates."

I carry two cups,
a pack of Thistle Shorties in Stewart tartan,
one of Nice Biscuits, the sugar gummed up
under the wrapper.

Sam looks up,
then down at Cartesian theory.
"Shorties or Nice?"
There's no other choice today.

K. V. Skene

All Roads Lead to Valletta

and the last *festa*
before the obligatory fast on Ash Wednesday
and the prayers and penances of Lent.
Slick in its orange and yellow livery
the oldest bus in the world ('Our Lady of Sorrows'
weeps over its windscreen.) creeps to the city gate
and Freedom Square's grandstand, ice-cream van,
street stalls – nougat, *figoli, Kinnie,*
and genuine leather caps. In Great Siege Square
all the café tables are taken and the tea
is English, the beer strong,
the wine cheap and cheerful
as the knee-high *maskarati*
giggling up and down
Byron's 'cursed streets of stairs'
and carnival's cartoons cascade,
splash old honey-stone walls
and dance-with-me music
you feel in the marrow of your bones
holds you – the sun in your eyes, a cool wind caressing
your body aching on the edge of it.

Figoli – an almond biscuit
Kinnie – a fizzy drink
maskarati – 'the masked ones'

K. V. Skene

You and I Pretty as the Morning

Once again the air is hot and heavy
down seven o'clock streets,
with the taste and smell of Mosta Market:
squid, eel, aubergine, olives, honey,
sweet buns with black coffee
in thick white cups
and the whine of morning traffic,
a wasp buzzing
long-winged, impatient
for nightfall, for the same old moon,
its soft light
becoming you.

Rope

Just a short length of frayed, cut-off rope;
cropped out one day, knee jammed at an edge,
my feathers flaring from the twine of threads,
or maybe later in the house of taupe
canvas, shielding him and Irvine; their hopes
waning, building with each day's fresh snow dredge.
That's how I've ended up here, one foot's breadth,
a splice unpicked from history, one wee grope
away from notes and letters on that climb,
hidden in his pocket until the rime
bound him, face-down to the mountain, hard
as marble, a cold bite freezing the damp
of fabric, drying, conserving his cramp
compressed into waiting out time's old guard.

Barbara Smith

Matches

We kept deep and dry in a leather pouch.
Pink tips on slight, square shafts – boxed Swan Vestas.
How many times had he cause to think us blessed,
when he'd spark one of us, in a low crouch,
to light the Unna cooker away from the reach
of the wind's whip, for snow-melt tea from the chest
kept far below at Base Camp, beside ours, wrested
all the way from Darjeeling, now beached
within the great array of boxes. Our small lights
for when the failure of days slid into starlit night
and calm air allowed a dozen tries for one match
to light the candle for a lantern show,
when each man jumped twelve feet into deep snow
and, as the candle died, found the fixed rope back.

from **The Sheep Fold**

Expectant

Child come of a snowflake,
you danced first in the cloud of a turning year
when only slightly bigger than a footprint.
Now lambs are thundering in wide spaces
you gallop and play inside,
with sharp movements, test how far you can shake me.
My life reshapes in your tiny unfinished hands.
I warm to the task in the rapid grass.
I knit the sun into small white sleeves.

                    *

Day by day, you brand your namelessness
upon my heart.
Night by night, my blood leaps
with your weight tied in me.
You curl your neat hips upwards;
rider in my belly,
cowboy of seahorses,
mermaid.
Lover of unknown gender,
do not rush to come into my arms.
I swell to the size of your life.

Keep me this way
as long as you want.

Transfusion
for the unknown blood donor

I left a dark flood
on the hospital floor.
The new blood
they cross matched to mine
is the bold colour of yours.
I want you to know
it helped me to breathe.

Strong now,
I take the baby in my arms,
and the gown of childbearing,
with its weight a sweat of moonstone,
slips from my shoulders.
Beneath I am naked as a ewe
that drops her fleece
at the clack of shears.

Released in this valley
rank with buttercups,
I feel your life love in me
strong as sacrament.

Sheepwash

Cob and thatch are normal here;
a chaffinch robs Jim's roof
for a bit of hi`s nest.
Jim says this week
is a case of corner hunting –
spring is round one of them.

Sunday morning
eases us into birdsong.
and I hear lambs
long before they come up the street;
my ears tuned to the sweet shrill pipe
of a newborn.

I lay our son between us,
untwine his soft limbs in sleep.
There is something of the mother
in that shepherd's voice.

Cum'on, Cum'on, Cum'on

Three hundred miles away,
my mother calls her ewes
and her mother, further,
in West Country dialect,
completes the ring
in the sheep fold.

Ruth Terrington

Trewellard

I prefer the old maps,
those that don't fit our envelopes nowadays.
We carried them in the Morris
that smelled of its own worn leather
and behaved like a person, hot and out of breath
by the time we reached Bodmin. Daylight was always
failing during that last push
out to the peninsula where everything resembled
something else: sheep like boulders,
disused tin workings like abandoned castles,
the sea a gauze wrap,
our village smaller than
its antique font on the Ordnance Survey,
children at dusk, and in the garden
a butt of green water
(its softness, my mother said,
owed to its source - a granite chamber).

The Child

in the gingham dress
is my mother, her mother,
my daughter, her daughter,
my self.

We sing with the one voice,
chant to the ball's thud,
skip rope's dry thwack.
We invoke boys: Adam to Zachary,
our futures hung on a name.

We rescue beetles, collect snails,
pedal trikes in white sun cotton
on pavements: Ballymacormick,
Ballygomartin, Buttermilk Loney.

Cats bask in flowerbeds.
Roses shower us with their gold.
Starlings' blether trickles from the sycamore,
and jackdaws jack-jack and chunter
contented on hot slate.

Judith Thurley

When the child asks
How do poems get made?
Does the sun sleep
in a cloud quilt?

Read her this.
Say to her, 'look love,
We have become a poem.'

Judith Thurley

Eleventh Night

Tonight in A&E
I need no thesaurus.
Speechless, breathing
stabs me in the back;
that dark bolus lodged
in my caved-in lung
might any moment obliterate
speech, breath, pulse, thought.

My right lung, once beautiful
and intricate as a sponge,
where blood jostled
to exchange gifts with the air,
is a dead space
clamped shut with pain.

A no-warning furore
of bawling henchmen
breaks out in the foyer -
shouts ricochet,
the staff nurse runs.

I am alone and the trolley sides are up.

Terror stalks the corridors
of my head -
things not done:
dishes, my unkissed sleeping children,
oblivious.
My funeral.

In my throat,
gasped monosyllables:
nurse
please
come

Palimpsest

Peeling back the walls,
like kneeling on the front step to peel potatoes,
inching off the crude-flesh wounds with a knife,
we find the ancestors of the house,

the notes and frail signatures of those
who regarded these rooms as their own,
and, taking their imprint with them in their minds
when they left, like a photo negative

left something of themselves to linger here,
a few words, a joke, a phone number,
which you know without calling
would ring for years off the hook.

We add our own, embarrassed by the marks
our hands make, blossoming out like mould,

like shapes in a corn-field, hieroglyphs that will one day
speak on our behalf like potato spores, code.

Salt

To meet with the 'tender-king of vegetables'
on his own terms is to be in step
with the seasons of marrow and Celsius

or so records the summer recipe section
of Hello! Magazine, its centrefold lascivious,
unspeakably green. I realise,

the last time I balanced on my tongue
the butter of its vowels was Madrid;
Asparagus week at the Prado Ritz.

The revolving door's gilt-edged pirouettes.
You eye the menu as a thousand green heads
bow down their necks,
I line up by height the condiments
and a waiter drops his pay-load of serviettes.

The Light-collector

I've been collecting pieces of light for years,
like scrap metal, in case one day we run out,
in case the moons bulb blows.

I lay traps for the night trains that stammer
along the old wooden tracks which lead away from the city
and into an unpolluted dark. I unclip windows,

like picture frames, from the walls of the houses
lit up in the distance.
I empty wing-mirrors, like fishing nets,

to see what they've caught in the night; peel
the moon from patches of water, like dried glue,
careful not to tear its blistered skin. I unpick stars

like stitches from sheets of disused glass
and place them into my breast pocket with the flint-sparks,
and strips of cotton laced with static. Then I head

home; unhooking the latches of intruder alarms
with an exaggerated wave as I run through gardens,
hopping fence after wooden fence, leaving my footprints

to glisten in the frost-bitten grass: following
the beacon of light that leaks through the gaps
in our loose tiled rooftop as it guides me home.

The Water–carrier

(i)
The calves are gone: all the cows, but one,
have been moved into the other field; the ghosts

of their cries, that went long into the night,
hang like mist on the air. The field has grown

in their absence, detail stitched into the unkempt
grass that wasn't here before: a cracked red bucket,

a silver feeding tray, wisps of wool and orange string,
snagged onto barbed wire. The cow that does remain is laid

out on the ground, where she's been for over a week
now; left for dead by the farmer who says he cannot afford

to have her put down. She doesn't acknowledge you, knelt
beside her, as you splash water from the dog's yellow

bowl onto her nose, her lips, as you do each day,
as you prolong her life in tongues of water.

(ii)
I throw the dog's orange Frisbee
towards the field's edge and watch it lose

its colour as it arcs across the sky.
The sun's imprint scatters amid the tall thistles

and discs of dry cow shit as i look away and find
you, in the distance, all over again: two silhouettes

among all the green and blue: at the point
where earth and sky collide.

(iii)
You're barely through the gate and from that distance
cannot tell the difference between life and death,

cannot see death's tiny detail:
the rusted edges of her closed eyes, the puss

that clings to her long lashes like dew to grass.
I crouch down and run my hands over her skin.

I can feel her warmth, each kink, each sharp knot
of bone beneath. I pull the dog away and shout

for you not to come over but you don't hear
me. You just carry on edging slowly towards us:

eyes fixed on the bowl of water cupped
in your hands; determined not to spill a drop.

Birth of a Naturalist

All century trash floated round the gyre
of the Pacific: bright and shiny, shoes
baked themselves open, grew weedy gills,
shoals of rolling bottles nudged each other,
blister packs burst delicately -
the scent of rubber curled itself round
chair legs like a cat.

   There were swirls of wilted condoms,
ribbed and stippled, a shining dummy teat,
slowly turning tyres: the stuff of shucked and
cast-off lives, cresting rills of milky foam,
breeding in long nests of hair.

   Worst of all in the warm thick clutter
were the shopping bags of every hue,
plaited together by the waves' regular hand
or domed, translucent as a bloom of medusae,
ripped membranes flickering like something precious.

   One day when the sky hung heavy,
I gunned the outboard motor, ducked the boom
to take a closer look. The brine was thick,
sounding a thin high note like a bell.

   The trash mass jostled for attention,
each piece sliding and mounting the other
as if silent hands pushed it out of the sea,
back into my hands, offering it up
and I knew that if I dipped my arm in
I would never get it back.

Crush

I was there, in his slipstream, as we wound
up the hills, over limestone pavements,
a rainbow crocodile of spotty geographers,
blisters throbbing on our heels.

He took me to Skelmersdale on the coach,
to Rio favelas, working slate mines.
I wondered if I could ever care
about maths or cross country again.

In Coniston, he tied my boots,
crossing the laces up my leg like a maypole.
The others laughed at my sudden interest
in cirques, my model of an oxbow lake,

the neat blue shading around Australia
but the A+ was a sign. I ran my fingers
over his worksheets, followed the kick
and curl of his hand - at night,

in my bunkbed, I walked the border
of his hairline, scaled the curve of his
canines till they grazed my knees.
I dreamt of his glass eye

Sarah Westcott

rolled under my pillow,
remembered the sundew we found
in Snowdonia - its beads of nectar,
the slow, dissolving flies.

Chloroxylonol

Before wood shavings or rubber under-swing mats,
before the soft, white-speckled tarmac,
before the rippled concrete that turned ice-glass in February,
there was grit:

the product of furnaces, making steel,
making all the hard products of the North West;
a cheap by-product in school playgrounds, underfoot,
in my scraped knees.

As the bandages came off, there were still
the small particles of pain, like the
darkened spot on the great red knee of Jupiter,
digging its way in.

Bathing was never the problem;
warm water soothed the jagged grounds,
as the kneecap healed and scabbed
around them.

It was the clean-sweeping smell of Dettol
– the cotton wool came soaked in it –
came to coax the grit bits from the cosy cushion
of my knee-flesh.

I'd rather then the tissue grow over and encapsulate,
so each small fragment would become me,
than feel the Dettol seeking out the septic grains,
slipping out sharp stones.

Hadrian's Brother

You should have seen his hen coop,
how he hammered posts,
knocked stakes and panels
a good foot underground.

No renegades would sack
a population in his care
and this held for the Brits;
Geordies through to Scousers.

"You can't divide a country up
like that", I said, but he had ordered
stone, enough to build a fair-sized city
and we had the apparatus

to layer blocks across
from Walsend (fitting name)
along the Whin Sill, Crag Lough
down to Bowness. That'll keep them out.

When he saw it, walked the length,
stopping at each mile castle,
he looked north at what the Empire
didn't want; "Scrub and Picts", he said,

but as he disappeared along the ridge,
as the neutral moon arced over,
a red dog fox was at the footings,
earth already flying from its paws.

Footings

Three years old -
you cast your expert eye
over the shallow footings
I have dug.
Your tongue concentrates
as you squat, squinting
along the tight, white line we pegged to mark the path.
Looking for the level
I shovel sand and gravel,
trusting that brick,
block and stone,
stamped by your shoes,
will bear weight when
you count the days
-    as I do.

Joseph

I

It was all tension
in the delivery room,
and you still seemed
glimpsed galaxies away,
pouring your heart out
in the automatic writing
of the foetal monitor's pen
that traced its racing.
 I heard each beat
as an outside broadcast
through a squeaky speaker
live-wired to your scalp. These electric things made more than a
potential difference
as the nurse noticed your distress.
The machine plotted nothing
and found its origin. Shocked into memory,
all I recalled was our first
virtual meeting in those
early scanning days when,
searched for like fish by sonar,
you showed up shadowy
in your secret space,
waving a hand to me

that could be a plesiosaur's paddle,
a coelacanth's fin - semaphore from
an oceans away womb-home, moon distant where you had landed.

Then, in the blink of an aeon,
you broke radio silence,
translating yourself again into the language of graph lines.

II

I saw you born from water
into air as you barged
into the summer. You were an astronaut to my eye,
space-walking from the mother ship
but blood-roped still, already miming our every voyage. It was
the quick slow motion
of it all that lives in me -
you coming from your sea of tranquillity,
washed up by the amniotic tide;
that suspended second when you looked
and held me in the forever of your face
before you drew breath,
before you cried.

George

I went to his cremation.
I remembered his nervous body.
I met his three fathers
and his three mothers
who had pinballed him
from house to house.

George from bondage
had delivered George
with a nylon rope
bought from a garage.
He slung it, hung from the neck.
The proprietor didn't know
that it would tow him somewhere else.

He had been discovered in his tree
by a dog and its woman.
The words had stopped in his throat;
the tongue was a bung,
swollen and blue in his face.
He swung like a clapper in a bell
but told nothing.

Low Dividend

It was just as I was beating
up the Yorkshire puddings,
and three weeks before I was rewired.
Back from the betting shop, he told me we had the pools up.
Twenty-three points. New carpet.
Dresses for the bairns.
Cortisone injections. Pigeons.
They kept his mind off things
at first.
But he went - with a hard winter,
and the smell of dinner
in the back kitchen.

Acknowledgements

Several of these poems have been published elsewhere prior to appearing in this anthology; the full details are not all available as we go to press and we acknowledge the work done by all the publishers involved in bringing some of this excellent poetry into the public domain prior to its reappearance here. We will add their website details to our links page in due course.

We also wish to thank and acknowledge all the writers who submitted their work to the 2010 Pamphlet and Collection Awards and thank the Judge, Pat Winslow. Templar Poetry also acknowledges the widespread support from many individuals and organisations throughout the British Isles and beyond who publicise both the Derwent Poetry Festival and the Templar Pamphlet and Collection Awards on.